BLACK IN N<

MARKETING, BRANDING AND SOCIAL MEDIA

Lisa Nicole Publishing
Lisanicolealexander.com
Gotha, FL 34734
Printed in the United States of America

ISBN: 978-1-7375515-8-4

Foreword

It's been one year since Blacks in Nonprofits was created, and what an amazing first year it has proven to be. Our platform on Facebook has grown to over 21,000 awesome nonprofit leaders of color from all over the world. The BIN Family, as I call it, was developed on the three basic principles of walking in love, operating with integrity and respect. Those three principles have shaped and molded our culture inside of our platform, and amazing things have happened since. One of those amazing accomplishments was releasing our first book within our series entitled Blacks in Nonprofits Grant Writers Edition that reached Best New Release and Best Seller on Amazon! YES, we were thrilled to make the list and empower so many black-led nonprofits with a dynamic resource to assist with funding, grant writing, and so much more!!

After seeing the huge impact the first book made, we brought another phenomenal group of experts together to produce the very first Blacks in Nonprofits Marketing Edition. Throughout our BIN platform, questions on how to properly market your nonprofit came up frequently, and we wanted to provide a hands-on resource guide to assist with this task.

Over the last year, I have had the absolute honor to meet and work with some of the most outstanding experts within the nonprofit sector. It has truly been a blessing and a dream come true to help people and connect them to tips, tools, and resources to take them and their nonprofit to the next level.

The authors who have contributed to this edition have put their heart and passion into creating a stellar book full of golden gems for successfully marketing your nonprofit organization. I am proud of them and the entire Blacks in Nonprofits Family for showing up each day and being the positive difference. We are changing our narrative in the nonprofit sector and educating black-led nonprofit leaders to be more productive and experience longevity with their nonprofits.

Dr. Rho

President and Founder
Blacks In Nonprofits

Table of Contents

Whit Devereux

info@whitdevereaux.com

FB: @whitdevereaux

IG: @whitdevereaux

www.whitdevereaux.com

Whit Devereaux is an Award Winning and Bestselling Author of "Not By My Own," "Unraveling the Layers: Memoirs of a Wounded Soul," "There's a Jewel in You, Volume 2," and "The Girl With The Crooked Smile." She is a Domestic Violence Survivor Advocate, Mentor, and Motivational Speaker. She is also the Founder and Executive Director of the 501 (c)(3) nonprofit organization **Not By My Own Community**, helping survivors of domestic violence to rebuild their lives by giving them a safe place to experience a life of wholeness through Jesus Christ.

Whit holds an Associate of Applied Science Degree in Paralegal Studies and a Bachelor of Arts degree in Applied Behavioral Sciences. She studied human behavior and has over a decade of experience working in social services settings. Through her company, Whit Devereaux Enterprises, she assists Entrepreneurs with obtaining sponsorships and gaining the attention of their target audience through media exposure and local partnerships. Whit has been featured on the cover story of the Chicago Defender, Soul 106.3, WVON Radio 1690, SHEEN Magazine, and is an active member of the Chicago Police Department District 006 Domestic Violence Subcommittee. Whit was recognized and awarded as one of the "Women Who Won in 2020" for the work she has done through her nonprofit.

As a mother of two, one of which she had as a teen mom, she enjoys taking family vacations, spending quality time with her daughters, and showing them that with hard work, faith, and determination - nothing is impossible. Connect with her via email at info@whitdevereaux.com or via the contact form on whitdevereaux.com.

PR Done Right

What is PR? According to PRSA.org, public relations (PR) is a strategic communication process that builds mutually beneficial relationships between organizations and their publics. A great rule of thumb to follow when it comes to **PR** is to remember that *integrity matters.* Yes, non-profits need **PR** too, in case you were wondering. When it comes to the best strategy for your non-profit, you must first consider: DIY or Hire? You may be wondering, "How do I even know if I need to hire a **PR** manager?" To assist your non-profit in making that determination, check for three key things:

1. You lack time to pitch yourself.
2. You have sent several pitches and have not gotten a response from anyone.
3. You have the budget set aside.

Hiring a dedicated **PR** Manager can yield a great return on your investment should you decide to hire out. However, if the three keys mentioned above do not apply to you and you have the time and skills to craft your own media pitches and secure placement, doing it yourself (DIY) may work out. The choice is yours, and the options are plentiful.

Relationship building is at the heart of **PR**. In general, individuals usually work well with those who they know, like, and trust. Look at really developing genuine relationships with the media contacts you make. When I was a freshman studying journalism at Columbia College Chicago, I had a teacher who gave me the best advice I have ever received regarding relationship building. She told the class: "If you're not networking, you're not working." As an introvert, the idea of networking initially made me cringe. What would I say? Should I bring someone with me?

However, you do not want your nonprofit to be a best-kept secret, so networking is certainly something you want to learn to embrace. One way to begin networking is to search the internet for events that are connected to your nonprofit mission or vision. Eventbrite and social media websites are great places to begin searching for keywords that resonate with you. For example, my nonprofit's mission is to serve domestic violence survivors. In months like October (Domestic Violence Awareness Month) and April (Child

Abuse Prevention and Sexual Assault Awareness Month), I search for the keywords associated with the month's themes.

Mutually beneficial partnerships matter and can come as a result of effective networking and relationship building. In a mutually beneficial partnership, both parties or entities benefit from working on a project, event, fundraiser, or other partnership. In doing my own PR work for my nonprofit and for the nonprofits I serve, whenever I sent a pitch, I was sure to include how working together would benefit our nonprofit in spreading awareness and how it would benefit the partnering agency. Some examples of mutually beneficial partnerships include but are not limited to exposure to a larger or new audience and increased awareness of mission, purpose, and efforts. Keep this in mind when reaching out to a person or organization. I get more responses when I explain how partnering with my nonprofit will help them as well.

Think outside the box! Promoting your nonprofit is something your organization, board, and volunteers should be doing regularly. It does not have to be difficult. Where do you spend the bulk of your time virtually and in person? Those are the places where you can share your mission with others. Virtual opportunities for promoting your nonprofit will be explained more in the next section, but old-school ways still work too! In my experience, we've reached greater success with our nonprofit campaigns utilizing both virtual and in-person tools. Even in the midst of a pandemic, you can still achieve success in promoting your nonprofit by using the options available to you.

If you spend a lot of time at the local grocery store, post your nonprofit flyer on their community board. If your nonprofit is near a library, contact them by phone and schedule a time to visit with your nonprofit flyer. You can also request to speak with the branch manager about developing a mutually beneficial partnership depending on what type of population your nonprofit serves (especially good for youth organizations). Once you have evaluated where you spend a majority of time and attention, it will be easier to execute a plan that best suits your nonprofit vision.

Using social media to build the buzz is absolutely a great FREE tool that nonprofits should use to promote their events.

Whenever our organization utilizes press releases or secures media coverage, we also use social media to share our messaging. Depending on the type of event or campaign your nonprofit is using PR for, it is best to begin earlier in your promotional efforts giving the organization at least six months to one year out for efficient planning. Don't have a social media page for your nonprofit? Why not? Are you worried about the cost? It's free and easy to set up. Stretched too thin already and don't have the time? As a nonprofit with 501c3 status, you can also use certain websites for free to help find a volunteer to help manage your social media pages (VolunteerMatch is one).

Keep this in mind when planning your next nonprofit event: Six months to one year of planning; utilize free social media tools and websites to build the buzz before, during, and after the event or campaign, and last but not least, make sure to thank your social media followers for supporting your mission. Once you teach your audience how to support your nonprofit (by liking the post, sharing the information, tagging a friend, donating, etc.), you will find that your social media followers (or family as I call them) will look for additional ways to support you. Educate them on your mission, vision, and progress made within your nonprofit community. People support those who they feel they like, know, and trust.

Press releases are still a great way to get your message out to the public. Some television stations and newspapers request them, and because you're reading this book, I'm going to give you a sample press release that you can customize and use for your next nonprofit announcement! I do it at least twice per year since our nonprofit host's bi-annual events, for example. You can submit a press release for your nonprofit as often as you have something that you want to share with journalists and your community. Word of mouth is still effective as well. Give your friends and family information that they can share with their friends and extended community. Some examples are brochures, flyers, business cards, and infographics.

Billboards are another creative way to share your nonprofit messaging. I've had one for myself and my client's nonprofits sharing what services are offered. Billboards usually consist of a logo, image of the community you serve, tagline (six words or less), and website. Phone calls are another avenue that hasn't gone away in the wake of technology. It is still a great way to connect your mission with real people who are also doing work that will be mutually beneficial.

Whenever I'm doing media outreach for nonprofits, I incorporate the three-contact rule. I learned this method when I was doing case management and have seen it be just as helpful when securing a placement. The method is to provide outreach using three different methods (if available) and/or three different attempts. For example, I email first, place a call next, then visit in person for specific clients. Sometimes emails go in the spam folder; individuals may not check their voicemails, or they are full, and in-person contact (masked up in this day in age) is still something companies can appreciate.

If those means aren't available, schedule at least three email attempts before moving forward. At the end of this chapter, you will also have access to a sample media pitch as a bonus thank you for supporting this book project! It is our hope to get you started on the right track with pitching and securing media placement to push your nonprofit awareness to the next level.

Using PR to generate recurring donors (email marketing, thanking/acknowledging donors, telling them how to support you) is also something I definitely recommend doing before, during, and after your nonprofit campaigns. It's like my mom always told me, "Being grateful makes room for more," so send out those thank you's! Using pop-up banners on your website teaching your audience how to support you with donations is a stand-out way to make your efforts known.

My nonprofit was recently approved for Google Ad Grants, and as a result, we were gifted with a $10K monthly grant budget and free marketing help to run ads. *Note if you have not applied for Google Ad Grants for your nonprofit now is the time. This creates traffic to your website, where you should have several calls to action for support, including a "Donate Now" button. Most sites allow you to embed this feature, or you can link it to outside sources such as PayPal Giving Fund for processing. As I mentioned above, once you have set up your website to accept donations or your social media page to accept donations, you can create email marketing campaigns, social media images, donation acknowledgment letters, and even a press release to increase your options for individuals and companies to bless your nonprofit with either monetary or in-kind (usually products or services) donations.

Always remember your why (mission). What is your nonprofit mission? This is what will encourage you on this nonprofit PR journey—keeping the mission the main focus will help you through tough seasons (we all have them). What is your mission? Are you just starting out? If so, create a mission that truly encompasses your why and include it in your PR strategy. For example, my nonprofit, Not By My Own Community Inc's mission is to help survivors of domestic violence rebuild their lives by providing a safe place for women to experience a life of wholeness through Jesus Christ.

Why is this important to me? I am a domestic violence survivor, and this is the ministry God gave me to serve His people. How will it help the community? Statistically, domestic violence affects one in three individuals, so we are all connected to someone who may need services. Preventing domestic violence and providing abuse recovery services is my PR strategy that intertwines with my why. Use my nonprofit why as a guide to establishing your own why, mission and the strategy will follow.

It goes down in the DM! Nope, it's not just a song, although it is pretty catchy. Great things can come from making contact through direct messages online. I must preface this by stating - do not spam people's inboxes with promotions. Remember we said earlier that it is important to establish mutually beneficial relationships? Whomever you are attempting to contact using DM should align with your mission and nonprofit campaign. Before hopping into their DM, you will have made a connection in other ways: supporting their mission, sharing their posts, engaging online - make it meaningful and genuine. People can spot opportunists a mile away.

If you see a company or influencer whose online presence resonates with your nonprofit goals - reach out, but do so in a very strategic, authentic way. I have made some amazing connections with people I've connected to using social media direct messaging. Give it a try and go in **expecting a yes.** Having this mindset of expecting a yes will boost your confidence in simply going for it! Something to note that I heard and absolutely love is if you happen to get a no, reframe the no as next. There's always something greater on the other side of next!

PR can be used for sponsorships also. A sponsor is an individual or organization that pays some or all of the costs involved in staging a sporting or artistic event in return for advertising. What are some duties of a Sponsorship Coordinator as it relates to PR? Nonprofit events can benefit from having sponsors to provide monetary and in-kind donations (services, products, etc.). With that said, a Sponsorship Coordinator will solicit sponsorship opportunities on your behalf. Often, they create sponsorship templates, sponsorship decks, and email templates to act on behalf of the nonprofit.

When you combine a sponsorship strategy with a PR strategy, you can ensure that your sponsors are getting what is outlined in the agreement (the deck should outline this in detail). Whether that be social media promotions, event shout-outs, signage at the event, logo on flyers, interviews online, etc., it will help push your messaging across the various platforms of the sponsor and vice versa as they will reach a new audience through sponsoring your event.

As with media pitches, I recommend that you reach out at least three times before moving on. There are plenty of organizations that are willing to support your mission and vision as a sponsor! Some sponsors I've built relationships with for clients and my own nonprofit include TGIN, Eden Body Work, PNC Bank, Palmers, Booty Bands, Suja Juice, and more! *Note: Taking my sponsorship deck to a meeting that I scheduled with my nonprofit bank led to me leaving out with $1000 in sponsorship. Contact your nonprofit banking institution to see what sponsorship opportunities they may have available in your area. Some creative ideas to find your next nonprofit sponsors are your business bank institution, small businesses in need of exposure, established businesses that align with your event, and target audience.

I got into PR by effectively managing my own book campaigns. I know you may be wondering by now what makes me qualified to speak on PR? I am an Author first and an Advocate next. When I was a freshman in college at Columbia College Chicago, I studied Journalism. I didn't get to finish because I was forced to drop out due to the high tuition costs and me being months pregnant with my oldest daughter. The dream did not die with me leaving the school. If anything, it birthed a researcher in me, and I became self-taught in marketing and promoting my own books years later. I also volunteered for my local church's domestic violence ministry, and there they taught me about using social media to reach your target audience.

I also believe in investing in myself, so I've taken classes and purchased products that not only help me but my clients as well. The first publishing company I used to publish my award-winning novel, Not By My Own, started referring aspiring authors to me who were looking for creative ways to market their books. Others saw the gift in me before I did. I would offer to teach those who reached out to me how to do it but instead, they wanted to pay me because of the success I had in managing my own book campaigns.

I am an avid learner, and everything I'm teaching you in this chapter is something that's been tested and has had significant results. In branding, marketing, and promoting myself, I learned the benefit of meeting the needs of other nonprofit leaders and social entrepreneurs through the use of PR. I absolutely love it and am passionate about getting the messaging across of those who are busy serving their communities. Everything I know is here for you to get a head start and if you stumble along the way, just reach out. I'm here.

How to find reporter's information: I know this is what you've been waiting for! (LinkedIn, tagged posts, FB groups, on news websites, Google "Chicago News Outlets") Since my clients are all over the globe, research is key in finding the right reporter for their specific project needs. I've found reporter's info through networking (yes - if you're not networking, you're not working, remember) in person and in social media groups, i.e., Facebook for PR professionals.

Again, you need to also bring something to the table in these types of environments. Give more than you take, and don't be afraid to ask for a contact. The worst they can say is no, but around here, we are expecting the yes! Another option is to literally Google "Your City News Outlets" and begin sifting through the search results for the ones that are closely aligned with your nonprofit mission.

I'm based in Chicago, so my search would yield results like Fox 32 Chicago, WGN 9 News, Chicago Tribune, Chicago Defender, Chicago Suntimes, and more. LinkedIn is another awesome opportunity to connect. Many media professionals put their contact information and/or title within their bio, so make the connection and follow up! A tip I've found most helpful is reading the tagged articles of outlets you've seen shared. There you will see the reporter's name and contact information, usually at the top or bottom of the article. From there, you can send a press release or media pitch directly to them via email.

Research what other media outlets similar nonprofits have been featured on to send your pitches to. Establishing your nonprofit as an agency that solves and addresses problems will keep you getting the right placements. Consider utilizing your current resources and connections. Who do you know that can connect you with the media? Chances are someone on your friend's list, colleagues, or acquaintances knows someone and would be willing to help you out. Simply ask. When drafting your media pitch, be cognizant of current events. If you see that the current media focus is equality and your nonprofit mission involves equality, edit your pitch to include this fact. Your pitch should be tied to what's going on around us. Relevant topics and actual results should be the focus.

Invest - you are/your mission is your greatest investment. Don't be afraid to invest in PR. Some agencies cost per hour, while others have monthly, quarterly, or annual packages. Compare agencies and have a budget in mind so that you can make an informed decision on choosing the option that is best for your nonprofit. Please know that PR is not an automatic money-making machine. Just because you've been featured on media doesn't mean you will get rich quickly. Be willing to invest your time, money, and energy into the PR process. It takes time for a media outlet to respond. If you think you're the only one reaching out to them on Monday at 9 am, I'm sorry to say, but you are mistaken. Their emails are flooded daily, and a successful PR strategy includes one that will help your nonprofit stand out. PR is a way to continually inform people on ways they can support the mission: volunteering, donating, attending events, sponsoring, partnering, sharing with others who may not otherwise hear about it. Remain open and participatory when working with a PR professional. I can't tell you the number of times people have invested the money for PR but not the time. Be sure that you can do both so that your nonprofit campaign can have optimum success. Because you have invested your time, money, and energy into purchasing this book, below are your bonus sample templates! I have personally used these for my clients. Feel free to edit and revise for your own nonprofit needs.

(MEDIA CONTACT INFO)
FOR IMMEDIATE RELEASE
June 26, 2020
MEDIA CONTACT
Whit Devereaux
Whit Devereaux Enterprises
872.221.0397
info@whitdevereaux.com

(HEADLINER) Courage Over Fear Productions Announces Face Your Fear, Face the World Campaign
(Sub-Headline) *Fifteen Days of Inspiration*
(Location)Chicago, IL (June 26, 2020) - (BODY INFO BEGINS) Courage Over Fear Productions will launch a fifteen (15) day Face Your Fear, Face the World Campaign, which will showcase videos and photos utilizing the hashtag #CourageOverFear of individuals across the world desiring to reset the second half of the year, starting on July 1, 2020. Aretha "Ms. Respect" Tatum, a minister and the director of Courage Over Fear Productions - a facet of Free Life - Life Changing Ministries, was led to create this campaign during this 15-day period to spread awareness and inspire others to enCOURAGE themselves. The campaign will run from July 1 - July 15, 2020.

2020 RESET - Let's start the second half of the year on a positive note! Now more than ever, the world needs to shift into a more loving, joyful, and positive space for us all to dwell! Join us! Post a picture or video of yourself with enCOURAGEing words for the WORLD. Use the hashtag #CourageOverFear.

(QUOTE Section) When asked about the thought of creating a movement of this magnitude, Aretha, the Creator of Face Your Fear, Face the World Campaign, states "I'm so excited about the upcoming #CourageOverFear Campaign! Everyone has different gifts, and mine is the gift of joy. I want to use this time to bring awareness, enCOURAGEment, and inspiration."

(Ticket Info/Any additional info) We want to see you! Submit your video or post using the hashtag #CourageOverFear on all social media outlets! Participants will be showcased on courageoverfear.org and Courage Over Fear Productions Facebook page.

(Reiterating Media contact information if someone wants to interview/cover) If you're a media outlet or photographer interested in covering Face Your Fear, Face the World Campaign, please send your inquiry to Whit Devereaux at info@whitdevereaux.com.

(BOILERPLATE) About Courage Over Fear Productions: Aretha "Ms. Respect" Tatum is a minister and the director of Courage Over Fear Productions, a facet of Free Life - Life Changing Ministries. Tatum is an award-winning filmmaker who uses film to ignite faith. She is also the author of two award-winning books, a motivational speaker, and a freelance writer with articles appearing in various magazines, including War Cry, a national publication of the Salvation Army. Courage Over Fear Productions mission is to uplift, encourage, and educate with faith-based seminars and special events.
###
(The "###" signs indicate the end of the press release)

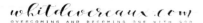
EMAIL SUBJECT: ATTN: Hank- Burst Into Books x Windy City Live Segment
GREETING Hello & Happy Monday Hank!

INFO - I hope that you had a great weekend! I am handling the PR for **Burst Into Books,** a nonprofit offering Literacy & Resources for children 6 months to 18 years old and providing representation by way of diverse authors, books & storytellers. We encourage and develop young readers to discover books, share stories, explore dialogue, and have fun! From youth book clubs, family events, writing workshops, educational services, and online workshops, you'll find plenty of inspiration for a great conversation and lots for your kids and families to get involved.

Since 2018, we've impacted over 2,000 young readers!

The nonprofit was recently selected for a $25,000 match grant and City of Chicago NOF grant and we are working to spread the message so more families can get the ongoing support services we've been able to provide thus far. With your help, we will be able to raise awareness to what is available and continue to remix the narrative, including adding after school programming! Burst Into Books can ease parental stress with their community offerings while keeping children engaged! With that said, I thought this may be a great segment and discussion for Windy City Live.

WRAPPING IT UP - Please let me know if you may be interested in the following suggestions below:

Interview with Creator of "Lit Talk" Online Educational Workshops (Discussing what attendees can look forward to)

- E-learning options to support parents and students through Burst Into Books
- Showcase Virtual Book Club and Highlight two of the Authors from "The Front Row" Virtual Author Story times
- **Online Community Town halls** *Discuss issues and solutions that will help rebuild our village (i.e., 2020 census, youth programming, fight against senseless killings, community organizing, mental health, etc.)

- Plans of expansion of programming as recipient of the City of Chicago NOF Grant

Looking forward to hearing back from you. Thank you!

-Whit Devereaux | @whitdevereaux | **www.whitdevereaux.com**

Rochelle Edrington

FB: @GrowWithVpro

IG: Grow.With.Vpro

LinkedIn: rochelleedrington

Info@MarketingVpro.com

Rochelle Edrington is a Client Attraction Consultant and owner of Vpro Marketing & Sales. She transforms meaningless marketing efforts into robust revenue-generating strategies for nonprofit founders, leaders, and consultants who want to show up and shine online while increasing their bottom line. Her data-driven strategies are designed to create consistent marketing, content, and sales outreach efforts that catapults cash flow.

Ms. Edrington does marketing from a sales perspective. She is a certified digital marketing specialist with 10+ years of sales experience and has a bachelor's degree in Marketing from Virginia Union University. When she is not growing her business, she spends time with one of her biggest champions and fiancé, Dewayne, and being a mother, judge, referee, and maid to her two preschool-aged daughters Nia Amor & Mya Destiny. She is passionate about entrepreneurship, women empowerment, self-development, and financial literacy.

Nonprofit Marketing Strategies

Online marketing was once an option for nonprofit organizations. With the decrease of in-person events due to the impact of COVID-19, leveraging digital marketing is mandatory for the survival of every organization, big or small. You may be thinking, "How in the world am I going to juggle program development, fundraising, board meetings, grant-writing, donor relations, and online marketing all at once?" Simple! Get guidance from an expert and lean on their knowledge and experience to educate yourself and your team or outsource those tasks. As a client-attraction consultant, I will share tips and strategies to help you show up and shine online while increasing your bottom line. You can lean on my experience and trust that you will complete this chapter with an understanding of how to align your marketing and content efforts so that you can focus more on your mission.

Nonprofits Changed My Possibilities

My parents kept my sisters and I involved in community programs. One of the organizations that really changed my life was Black Achievers. They took inner-city high-school students on a five-day HBCU college tour across five states. I could clearly see the possibilities of attending college, despite my surroundings. In my 20s, nonprofit organizations helped me fill the gap when I fell on financial hard times and needed help paying my utilities and rent. The work of nonprofit leaders, such as yourself, is partly why I am who I am today. I am dedicated to assisting nonprofit professionals with changing or creating new possibilities within their organizations, so they can continue to do the real work in the field and invoke change in our society.

Disconnect Between Nonprofits and Their Communities

I was collaborating with a nonprofit consultant when I witnessed a serious disconnect between nonprofits and the communities they endeavored to reach, and that disconnect was marketing.

Organizations could not:

1.   Reach their audience

2.   Attract financial supporters

3.   Recruit board members and volunteers

It all boiled down to the two essential pillars of business and marketing:

1.   Understanding your target audience

2.   Communicating value

Too often, nonprofit leaders begin to promote their organizations before understanding who they are talking to or why they should care. This is the #1 culprit of ineffective marketing efforts. If you do not know who you are talking to, and don't know how to get their attention, then you are merely talking to yourself. It's like giving directions to someone who doesn't speak your language. Even with good intentions, how helpful was the information? Probably not much.

Before You Begin Marketing Online

Before you begin marketing online, know what you want your results to be. You need to:

1.   Set clear goals. Examples of clear goals are raising awareness, acquiring new donors, improving community engagement, and becoming a go-to resource. Make sure that your marketing goals are in alignment with your business goals.

2.   Understand who you want to attract. Know your target audience. Your message is not for everyone. When you speak to everyone, you will grab the attention of no one. Understand the basic demographics of your audience, such as gender, income, race, location, and age. You should also know their goals, values, pain points, and challenges. Most importantly, understand why they chose to support your organization. When you put all this information on a document, this is called creating an avatar. Center your marketing communication around your avatar to increase the likelihood of attracting ideal supporters.

3.   Develop a value proposition. You need to communicate your organization's value and why someone should care. To do so, concisely answer:

○   What problem do we solve?

○   How does this benefit our audience?

○   Why should they support our organization instead of the organization down the road?

4.   Provide a place to consume content. Once you show up online, you will need to have somewhere to send people who are interested in learning more about your organization. This could be your website, blog, social media page, newsletter, etc. Not everyone will be ready to donate to or support your organization after the first connection. Therefore, offer a space where they can consume content and stay connected.

Nonprofit Marketing Strategies

What is a marketing strategy? A marketing strategy is a game plan to reach prospective consumers and convert them into customers—or, in your case, to financial supporters. The three essential components of a nonprofit marketing strategy are a website, a newsletter, and social media. When you develop a system that positions you to connect with your audience and convert your followers into supporters, you will see the results you want.

Build Your Website

By now, I hope you have a website. I know sometimes there are differing opinions on whether a new organization needs one. I'm a firm believer that if you are entering this industry for the long term, then get one. Every organization's goal is to attract new people outside of its network. But if someone wants to research you first but can't locate you, how likely are they to invest in your mission? Not likely. Get a website!

Just so you know, wix.com gives substantial discounts for nonprofit organizations. As of 2021, they will give up to 70% off a two-year subscription.

Their platform has a drag-and-drop feature that helps a novice feel like a pro. If you don't want to create it yourself, connect with me to create a professional online image.

Website Call to Action (CTA)

Have you ever gone to a website, and you've been there only two or three seconds, and something pops up that wants you to take action? It's called a pop-up box. That's what I want you to add to your site. Your call to action can be to subscribe to a newsletter, donate to your page, or register for your next event(s). According to Small Business Trends, 70% of small businesses lack a call to action. According to Grafton, users spend only about 5.59 seconds looking at a website made up of written content, and they spend about 5.94 seconds looking at a website with a main image.

Knowing this, you should capture their attention within the first 2-3 seconds with a call to action, so your efforts to drive traffic to your website can be quantified. Add a newsletter sign-up box to capture emails. If you offer free downloads, be sure to ask for their email address; this will also help grow your list.

Develop a Blog

Not too many organizations leverage a blog, but a blog is a great way to keep your audience informed, attract more people to your website, and leverage the power of SEO. With the right keywords in your blog, Google will begin to allow your site to show up on the first page of the search engine. Please understand, SEO is a long-term game. Blogs can also help develop content for your newsletters. Whenever you're creating a blog, you can launch a newsletter to let your audience know about a new blog you just posted.

A couple of nonprofit blog ideas are:

1.   Upcoming events

2.   Success stories

3.   Introducing volunteers, staff, and board members

4.   Answering frequently asked questions

5.   Giving insight into your industry

6.   Sharing the impact of donations

7.   Giving insight into your partners

8.   Thanking current donors

9.   Telling the story of your nonprofit

10.   Sharing how people can show their support

There are so many other ideas, but these are just to get you started.

Start a Newsletter

People buy from those they know, like, and trust. Utilize your newsletter to build trust. According to M+R benchmark reports, 13% of online revenue comes from email messaging. Let's maximize this opportunity to convert your followers into financial supporters. The most valuable content from newsletters is created with your avatar in mind. Speak to their challenges, values, pain points, or goals.

Here are a few things that you can also include in your newsletter:

1.   What's New

2.   Upcoming Events

3.   Staff Spotlight

4.   Volunteer Spotlight

5.   Nonprofit Milestones

6.   Progress Report

7.   Tips & Advice

8.   A Message from Leadership

MailChimp, Constant Contact, Active Campaign, Campaign Monitor, and Mailer Light are some of the most popular platforms for email marketing. When you create your newsletter, please make sure you have a call to action (CTA) in every email. You want your audience to take action by clicking a button or clicking a link. Every platform will have analytics. These analytics will allow you to see who opened your email and who clicked. This will inform your next plan of action.

Segment Your Mailing List

Segmenting means separating your mailing list based on commonalities to create a personalized experience. When an individual feels like you are talking to them personally, it helps build trust because they feel like you know and understand them. When your audience trusts you, they are more likely to become a contributor.

Segment your list into:

1.   Past donors

2.   Current donors

3.   Board members, staff, and volunteers

4.   Event attendees

5.   New email subscribers

6.   Non-donors

7.   Partners

Social Media

If you do not have a team, do not spread yourself thin in an attempt to be present on every platform. Choose the platform where your audience hangs out. Do understand, the platform where your clients hang out could be different from the platform where your financial supporters' hang out. For example, let's say you had a program for black girls interested in entrepreneurship, and the girls' parents were from age 35-45. There is a huge chance that your potential clients (i.e., their parents) hang out on Facebook.

Let's say your financial supporters are business owners. There's a higher chance the business owners would be on LinkedIn.

Post Frequency & Timing

If your organization has less than 10K followers, and you find your marketing efforts to be inconsistent, a good rule of thumb is to start by posting every other day (i.e., 15 times a month) at a minimum, with the goal of eventually getting to the point where you post once a day. Your analytics on any social media page will typically tell you at what times your audience is online. Utilize that data to direct your posting times.

Content Marketing & Awareness

One area that many seem to overlook is developing a content marketing strategy. A secret weapon for nonprofits is to really jump on the bandwagon of "awareness" days/months/weeks. Choose an awareness theme (i.e., Cancer awareness month, entrepreneurship month, financial literacy, etc.). Show how the chosen theme impacts who you serve. Most of the time, national organizations will also have social-media kits available that you can use. Leveraging this strategy will help you increase awareness about where your organization stands on those topics.

Drive Traffic

You want to drive people from social media to your site. This is extremely important. One of the biggest mistakes that businesses make is they spend a lot of time building their following and engagement on social media, but they never find a way to get their followers away from social media and into their own assets. What I mean by "asset" is your website and/or your newsletter—something that you own, something that is yours.

Social media and all these other distribution points are rented spaces. What happens if you invest your time building a highly engaged Facebook page, then Facebook decides to cancel your page because you violated one of the rules you were unaware of? Now, you have lost all those years of hard work. That is what I mean by "rented space." You don't own it. So, please find a way to get more connected and convert your followers to your own assets.

Facebook Ads

If you want to use Facebook Ads and the Boost feature, then make sure that you understand your target audience.

When you have an avatar, you can use the details from the avatar to learn how to do your Facebook ads. For example, your avatar may show that your target audience is made up of Black women between the ages of 25-35, living in Harrisburg, Pennsylvania, mostly in nursing, and are interested in entrepreneurship. So when you use Facebook Ads Manager, you can dig down and make sure that only those women will see your ad. The Boost feature will not allow you to enter their occupation or interests, but you can still enter their age, location, and gender. Remember to use your avatar to inform you in every area of your marketing strategy.

Maximize the Google Ads Grant

What's the Google Ads grant? Well, Google offers $10K in advertising for nonprofit organizations. Whenever you're launching a campaign, and you want to maximize your reach, you can utilize the Google Ads grant.

It is very beneficial if your organization offers products or paid services because it can catapult your volume of customers. On average, small-to-medium-sized for-profit businesses spend about $9K-$10K a month on advertising.

Most nonprofits cannot afford that, so Google gives you a resource to compete with small-to-medium-sized businesses as it relates to advertising space. It's a huge opportunity to generate traffic, income, and revenue for your organization that is often overlooked. If this is something that you want to use for your organization, please connect with me. My information is at the end of this chapter.

Marketing Campaigns

What is a marketing campaign? A marketing campaign is a planned, organized sequence of activities designed to bring in revenue or awareness, often leveraging several different channels.

A campaign can benefit any organization that has a goal to:

1. Promote new services, programs, and/or products

2. Grow an online presence

3. Generate leads and/or donors

4. Reach a new audience

5. Engage with existing supporters

6. Increase revenue and/or

7. Acquire new donors and/or members.

Campaigns typically run for about 30-45 days.

T-Shirt Fundraising Campaign

Many people in this space have often decided to run a t-shirt fundraising campaign. Some bypass this option because they feel like there are other fundraisers that can yield a higher return. However, do not overlook t-shirt fundraising because it can help convert your followers into financial supporters. The benefits of t-shirt fundraising are building a connection with your community and building your donor list. A donor can buy a shirt for $25. If you nurture that relationship over time, that $25 donation can then be converted into a $250 donation, which can then be converted into a $2,500 donation. Always start with the end in mind!

When you sell shirts, you now have walking billboards. When others are wearing a shirt that is visually appealing or has a thought-provoking or inspirational statement, anyone who sees them wearing it will ask about it. Where did they get it from? What does it stand for? At that moment, you will have created someone who will spread the message of your organization. It's like creating a whole team of salespeople!

T-shirt fundraising can improve engagement with your staff, board members, and volunteers. It can build excitement for your goal. It's human nature; people love to help. So, you should maximize that theory to leverage your campaign. It also builds brand advocates. It expands your brand awareness, expands your visibility, and monetizes your marketing efforts.

Here are the foundational steps to launching a social-media t-shirt fundraising campaign.

4-6 weeks out, you need to:

1.   Set a launch date

3.   Identify your message

4.   Set smart goals

5.   Define your target audience

3-4 weeks out, you need to:

1.   Create content

2.   Schedule posts

1-3 weeks out, you need to:

1.   Promote and network

2.   Analyze your analytics (make sure to do this while your campaign is running, too!)

If you want to launch your t-shirt fundraising campaign and receive marketing support, then an awesome platform to use is www.Campaign4ACause.com. This platform is black-led and owned by yours truly, me! Nonprofit organizations can launch their t-shirt fundraising campaigns on the site with no upfront cost, no inventory, and no delivery headaches, all while receiving free marketing support during their campaign and in the Facebook group. In addition to this campaign, if an organization wants to receive high-level marketing training, they can enroll in the 3 hour "Social Media Fundraising Campaign" paid workshop to learn how to implement and promote the campaign.

Make Time for Online Marketing

When it comes to online marketing, there are a few areas you will need to make time for, such as creating posts, curating posts, and analyzing content.

Consider breaking your time into blocks in which you do each of these tasks or set one day aside to knock everything out. Online marketing (and marketing in general) is a long-term game.

With the many things you have going on, it is easy to get distracted and become unproductive, but we both know that marketing is essential to your organization's growth. Remember your "why." Make a list of why it is important for your organization to be seen by the masses. What impact can it make? What lives can it change? Write down your "why" and keep it in front of you.

When you are feeling discouraged or disconnected, reconnect with marketing education for inspiration. Fill your mind with the knowledge you need. It can open your creative channels and give you a new perspective. Join supportive communities that will be a shoulder you can lean on during those times. Remember that your commitment to implementing a consistent online marketing strategy will lead to the five C's: clarity, confidence, clients, contributors, and cash flow.

Now, what are you going to do with all the knowledge you learned from this chapter? Take this time to write down how you want to implement what you have learned.

Answer these questions:

1.   What strategy do you want to implement?

2.   What could prevent you from maximizing this strategy?

3.   How will you overcome it?

When convincing yourself, your board members, or your staff, remember that online marketing provides real-time results. Unlike traditional marketing, where you must kick out a bunch of money and sit with your fingers crossed, hoping that you will get results during a campaign. Check out the analytics and see how things are going, and if it's not going right, then you can change it, or you can stop a campaign that's costing you too much. Online marketing is beneficial, but you need to clarify your audience and what strategy might be best for your organization.

If your organization is at the point where you would prefer to hire a consultant to come in and provide their services, then visit my website **www.MarketingVpro.com** and let's book a 60-minute consultation to discover how we can transform your marketing efforts into a revenue-generating strategy.

If you're ready to launch a t-shirt fundraising campaign, then visit:

www.Campaign4ACause.com.

I hope that during our time together, you were inspired to transform

something in your business. Let's continue to grow!

Terrence Green Jr.

YouTube: TJ's Animation Workshop

FB: @TJsAnimationWorkshop

IG: @TJsAnimationWorkshop

www.TJsAnimationWorkshop.com

TJ@TJsAnimationWorkshop.com

Terrence Green Jr. considers himself to be a visual storyteller. What began as an English project is starting to change the way nonprofit organizations communicate their message. Terrence makes animated videos that catch people's attention and also keeps it until the very end. He believes that animated videos are the perfect way to tell your story, break down complex messages, and attract more eyes to your organization. He studied different areas of marketing so that his videos would be more effective.

Terrence uses a four-step process that he talks about in his chapter that makes the process smooth from start to finish. He also created a course that teaches people how to make animated videos themselves. In this chapter, he discusses what animated videos are, how they can help you reach donors or partners, how to get started, and even compares the pros and cons of hiring someone or doing it yourself.

Telling Your Story Using Animation

What is animation?

Do you remember those Saturday mornings as a kid when you grabbed a bowl of your favorite cereal and got in front of the tv to watch your favorite cartoons, whether it was Tom and Jerry, The Jetsons, or the Flintstones? Those are examples of animation. There are different types of animation. There are 2D, 3D, whiteboard, animated explainer videos, cartoons, etc. Animation is popular because it is attractive, and things can happen in animation that can't happen in real life. Things like Tom chasing Jerry and falling off a cliff or Bugs Bunny getting hunted by Elmer Fudd.

The limitless possibilities in animation alone make it potentially satisfying. In this chapter, we will talk about how animation can be used to tell the story of your organization and how that will help you grow your nonprofit. The form of animation we are going to be focusing on is called *animated explainer videos*. Animated explainer videos help you explain an idea, organization, process, etc.

For example, suppose you have an organization that helps domestic violence victims. Your video could include the problems victims face, the percentage of families that are impacted, the solutions you have to help these victims, why your organization is unique, the resources and benefits you provide, and the process people would go through to reap the benefits that you offer.

Why animation?

Animation is attractive and engaging. People tend to fall in love when they see an animation. It's hard to explain why, but I think the story of how I started will give you a good example of what I mean. When I was a senior in high school, we had a project about William Shakespeare. We had to either work with a group to reenact one of his plays or work alone and record ourselves pretending like we are interviewing him. Well, months before that, I stumbled upon this software where I could make animated videos easily by just dragging and dropping. So, when the project came up, I instantly had an idea and asked the teacher if I could make an animated video of me interviewing him.

I had no experience with the software or animation, and don't forget I was still in high school. The video took about a weekend to create, and to make a long story short, the class and the teacher loved it. I ended up getting a 98/100 on my project. The only reason I didn't get a hundred was because the video didn't really include any Shakespeare facts like it was supposed to. To be exact, in the video William Shakespeare came out and after I introduced him to my animated audience. I asked him one question, then the studio caught on fire, and William Shakespeare helped me put it out.

The teacher loved the video so much that she showed it to her four other English classes. You see, people just fall in love with animation. It triggers something in the brain. It takes away the reality effect because we know anything can happen in the video. When I show someone my animated video, ten times out of 10, I see their face light up with a smile. This was the first animated video I created! I would later go on to make another animated video years later for an app I was trying to create. It was at the moment I decided to start making animated videos to see if I can turn it into a career.

This is just one of the many examples that showed me that people absolutely love animated videos, even if they consisted of the simplest things. But the question is, why? Well, to be honest, this question doesn't just have one answer. From my five-plus years of personal experience, I can tell you that when I told people I made animated videos, they were intrigued 99% of the time. It was very rare that I would come across someone who didn't like the fact I made animated videos or like the videos that I made.

Animated videos automatically attract people to you, and it keeps them there. Animated videos keep people engaged in the message to keep them watching and receive what you want to tell them. Three ways that animated videos engage people:

1. Anything can happen
2. Animated videos can break down complex messages
3. Animated videos can tell a story

Animated videos can accomplish anything you can imagine (depending on the skill level, we will talk about that later). You can have a rocket blasting off, someone jumps into a volcano and appears in the next scene, you can fight a bear, tiger, and lion and still win.

Just let your imagination run wild. Any point that you want to make, you can make with animation. Can you say you can do that with other marketing tools?

How can you attract donors and partners?

When it comes to attracting people to you, you need to make sure that you are catching their attention. You do that by communicating messages that matter to them at that time. That can be solving a problem, addressing a need, or speaking about something that interests them. Let's think about it like this. Imagine that you are driving in your car, and you have been on the road all day and haven't eaten, and you come across three billboards.

One billboard is advertising an automotive shop that can fix your car in an hour no matter the problem. Another billboard is advertising a big sale on clothes. The last is advertising an all-you-can-eat buffet. Which one is more important to you at that moment? Of course, it will be the buffet because your current state is hunger, and that is the message that relates the most to you.

No matter how good the service is at the automotive shop or how good the deals are for the clothes, your mind only remembers and pays attention to what matters to you at that point in time.

It's the same thing when you are trying to reach your target audience; the message needs to relate to them. So, before you even make a video, you need to figure out who it is that you want to attract. Say, for example, you are trying to attract donors for your organization that helps youth get into the college of their dreams. We are going to call our imaginary organization, Path to College. You need to explain to donors what barriers keep our youth from getting into colleges.

You would need to explain that if they have certain tools, it could increase their chances of getting into the college of their dreams. What makes your organization unique? How does it help accomplish the goal of getting youth into their dream colleges? What will you need from them to help you accomplish this goal? How will their gifts be used to help accomplish this goal? This can all be included in the initial video.

In later videos, you can show that since your organization has started, college acceptance rates have increased for the youth in the community, and more of the youth are getting the jobs they are interested in. Your organization has had a snowball effect on the next generation of youth. If you are targeting partners, there will be similar messages like what barriers are there, the tools that increase their chances for college, and what makes your organization special.

The main differences in the videos will be where you talk about the positions you are looking for help in, how you plan on growing the organization with the help, and more. The goal is to think about what general questions the audience you are targeting may have and answer them in the video. This is why it is important to target a specific audience in a video because donors may have different questions than partners. But the positive side is that the information is the same for both. If this is new to you, it may be a bit confusing, so we will go over a script for the organization we made up, Path to College. Script one will target donors, and script two will target partners.

Script one:

There are a lot of things the youth in our community have to give up, but college should not be one of them. Not every child has the same opportunity to go due to a lack of funds, guidance, or support. This is why we started Path to College. We build a foundation under our youth to make sure they are able to go to any college they please.

We do this by taking care of half of their tuition if needed, setting them up with a mentor that can help them decide what college they would like to go to based upon the career path that interests them, and a support system that will make them feel like they can do anything. Our staff of volunteers is full of individuals from the education system, and we are familiar with the path it takes to not only get to college but get through it as well. With your donations, we can increase the number of youth in our community that we can help send to college and begin their lives. For more information on how to donate, please visit our website.

Script two:

There are a lot of things the youth in our community have to give up, but college should not be one of them. Not every child has the same opportunity to go due to a lack of funds, guidance, or support. This is why we started Path to College. We build a foundation under our youth to make sure they are able to go to any college they please.

We do this by taking care of half of their tuition if needed, setting them up with a mentor that can help them decide what college they would like to go to based upon the career path that interests them, and a support system that will make them feel like they can do anything. We are looking for volunteers that have experience in the education system so that we can help guide our youth in the direction they would like to go. We want to help them create a plan and support them along their path. We plan to continue to grow and hope to have enough volunteers to get each child in our program a mentor that will be with him all the way until they graduate. For more information on how to get involved, visit our website.

As you can probably tell, the first part of the script was exactly the same. The difference came when we were describing what we were looking for from our audience; and that is how it looks when you are creating a video for different audiences. It doesn't have to be a big change but make sure you are talking to that specific audience to increase your chances of success.

That is why it is very important to know about your target audience. I am not simply talking about what they care about because you are trying to attract people who care about the same things you care about. I am talking about questions they would have, the information they would need to decide whether to support you, how long it usually takes them to make a decision, etc. Knowing all of this will help you build a video that will get and keep their attention and a compelling video that will get them to take action.

Getting started

Now how does storytelling relate to any of this? Stories help us relate to the message. It helps us connect point A to point B, and it helps to make sense of things.

We naturally love stories, and we have ever since we were little. At the beginning of the chapter, we talked about how we loved cartoons as kids; well, they told us stories. We even like stories now. We get them from our favorite TV shows, movies, or books. Stories help us relate to the main character, and we follow them along with the storyline. It puts us in their shoes. It even helps us get a clearer understanding of what someone is saying.

For example, have you ever been confused or lost on what something meant, then someone gave you a good example, and it was like an aha moment of realization? You were probably like, oh, I get it now. It's like they painted a picture in your head. That is the feeling you want to give your target audience. You want to paint a clear picture for them. You want them to understand your message, your organization, what it is that you do, and more.

I have no doubt in my mind that your organization is making or going to make a difference in your community and the world. But in order to grow and get the resources you need, you need to be able to communicate your message to others clearly. You want to put them in the shoes of the people you are trying to help or the goal you are trying to accomplish.

Using stories to put your audience in someone else's shoes brings out empathy in them. This is where the combination of storytelling and animation comes into play.

Earlier, we talked about the benefits of animation and how it breaks down complex messages and makes them simple. It also amplifies the message, and the visuals make them stand out. We just talked about how stories help people relate to the message and step into someone else's shoes. That is what we call animated storytelling. Now you know what animated storytelling is and how it works. Next, we are going to talk about how you can apply it to your nonprofit organization. We are now going to create a nonprofit organization and market it with animated storytelling.

Our nonprofit will be called "Entrepreneurs of the World," where we help entrepreneurs and small businesses get off the ground through funding and expert guidance. Every time I create a video, I go through the same four steps.

- Gathering Details
- Create a Plan
- Execute
- Examine and Adjust

We mentioned gathering details earlier when we talked about knowing who the target audience is and what the message is you want them to receive. Before you do anything, you need to sit down and put the information you need in front of you. When you are gathering details, there are six things that you need to know. Depending on the project you are doing, there may be more, but at the very least, you need to have these six things.

1. Target Audience

2. Problem

3. Solution

4. Why are you/organization important?

5. What is the process?

6. Call to Action -What do they do next?

I learned this process from creating animated videos. When I first started making videos, I would go into the software and start working on the video without any plan or idea of how I wanted the end result to look. This would lead to getting lost on what I wanted to do, going back to earlier parts to change things around, and getting frustrated throughout the entire process.

It got the job done at the end of the day, but I didn't realize there was a much easier, less stressful way to do it. Then I started writing out the script and drawing out the animation I wanted to go with each sentence. This did three things for me. **The first thing** was that it was faster in the long run. Because again, I would start making scenes, and as I got further into the video, I would realize something didn't look right, so when I changed it, I would have to go back to later parts in the video and change them as well because they were either a continuation of the mistake I just corrected or did not fit the video anymore.

So now, when I start planning, I take a step back, look at it from the view of the entire video, and not just focusing on one scene as I go. **The second thing** it did for me was, it prevented me from procrastinating. Have you ever had so much to do that you ended up doing nothing at all? I would go through the same thing. Videos would take me so long that I would dread having to create one, especially when I had multiple videos to create. But when I implemented my video-making process, it broke down each part of the video and allowed me to look at the video as different pieces rather than an entire video.

My chemistry teacher would always tell me that the only way to eat an elephant is piece by piece. This process helped me chop up my elephant. **The third thing** it did was help me make better quality videos. I broke down each step, and now I could focus solely on that step. When I was writing out the script, I could solely focus on the message. And when you can put your focus on one single thing, it will naturally be better. The same happened when I was creating the animation since I already knew what I would put in each scene. I could focus on making my animation creative and smooth.

When I first started creating animated videos for people, I realized that they didn't know exactly what they wanted when they came to me. They just knew that they saw the animated video and wanted it for their organization. So when they would take some time to try and figure out what they wanted, it would go from taking days to taking weeks to them not getting a video because they didn't know what they wanted. So I made a questionnaire with these exact questions to get the details they needed to write a script for them.

For example, if we wanted to create an animated explainer video that introduces our organization to donors, here is what our form would look if we were to fill it out for our nonprofit organization.

1. **Target audience:** Donors

2. **Problem:** It is difficult to start a business without funding or previous business knowledge.

3. **Solution:** An organization with financial resources and access to the industry professionals.

4. **Why is our org important:** We have staff with business experience and a network of companies in different industries.

5. **What is the process:** Business owners interested in applying for grants or mentoring can sign up on our website. They will then meet with one of our ambassadors, who will examine what stage the company is in and then the steps they need to take moving forward. To donate, go to the donate tab on our website and either become a regular donor or give a one-time gift.

6. **Call to Action (What does your target audience do next?):** Visit our website to donate or become a partner.

As we talked about earlier in this chapter, the message, no matter who you are targeting it will be the same. Therefore, your details will look the same whether you target donors, partners, or the people you are helping. In this specific detail form, our target audience is donors. The problem is the *issue* that we want our target audience to be aware of. This is how we are going to relate to them and get their attention. The solution lets the audience know, that there is hope to solve the problem. We want them to stay to learn more about what we have to say. This is going to show them that we are serious.

Number four is going to talk about why they should believe in us. Why are we the best organization to carry out this solution, and why we deserve their hard-earned money. After that, we want to talk about what the process looks like for people who are interested in our organization. You can also speak about the process of how donors can give money to our organization. Finally, in every advertisement you do, you want there to be a call to action. You want to lead your target audience to a specific place.

This is important because people watch videos all the time on Facebook and then go to the next video. You want them to pause and take action now. This action could be to lead them to subscribe to your YouTube Channel or other social media. Even if they don't donate now, they can continue to follow your nonprofit and donate later and reshare content to other potential donors.

Now how did I create a script with this info? I utilized the questionnaire because it is the details part of the process. Now we move on to the planning part of the process; This includes scripting and storyboarding the video. Check out this short script using the details I filled out for our new nonprofit, "Entrepreneurs of the World."

Three hundred businesses each year in our community shut their doors due to a lack of money. But what if they had an organization in their community that could not only provide financial help but industry expertise as well. That is why we started Entrepreneurs of the World with a staff of over 50 years of combined business experience. We could use you to join a group of investors that want to give back to our community. To learn more and donate, go to www.Entrepreneursoftheworld.com to get started.

Now let's break down the script to see how I used the details we wrote down. *"Three hundred businesses each year in our community shut their doors due to a lack of money"* is where we addressed the problem. We put it in a way that will attract the people who care and raise alarms. We want to bring attention to an issue quickly so they can stop scrolling on social media and hear us out. *"But what if they had an organization in your community that could not only provide financial help but industry expertise as well."* This sentence is where we introduce the solution we have for the problem. *"That is why we started Entrepreneurs of the World with a staff of over 50 years of combined business experience."*

In the next sentence, we introduce ourselves and briefly explain why we are the right organization to trust in helping out with the problem. "W*e could use you to join a group of investors that want to give back to our community."* Most scripts will probably address the target audience at the end when they want them to take action or when the video is mentioning where the person who is watching the video comes into play. But it is also common for the target audience not to be mentioned in the video.

You will mainly want to know who your target audience is so that you can address the message in a way they can relate to. *"To learn more and donate, go to www.Entrepreneursoftheworld.com to get started."* And last but not least, this is your call to action.

This is usually the formula for most scripts. Remember that each video is targeting different people, and it needs to speak to that target audience. Before you write a script, pay attention to what you want to say, how you word it, the flow, and what type of emotion you are trying to pull out of the viewer. Even when you get stuck while writing your script, you can get inspiration from watching a few online videos. Your script will be your foundation for your video, so you need to make sure it is solid.

Now we move on to storyboarding the script. Storyboards are drawings or explanations of the animations you will use with their corresponding sentence(s). This is important because this is where you let your mind run free and plan out your video. Once it's time to create it, you have an idea of what you want it to look like. Take a look at the storyboard I created for our nonprofit.

Three hundred businesses each year in our community shut their doors due to a lack of money.

Animation: The scene starts out with a group of businesses on the screen with the number 300 above them. Then they start to fade away toward the end.

But what if they had an organization in your community that could not only provide financial help but industry expertise as well.

Animation: 2-part split-screen – the same character on both sides, the one on the left is shaking hands with someone in a bank, and the one on the right is in a meeting with a group of business people in suits.

That is why we started Entrepreneurs of the World with a staff of over 50 years of combined business experience.

Animation: The organization's logo flashes on the screen, and then it transitions to a scene where the camera pans a line of people slowly from left to right.

We could use you to join a group of investors that want to give back to our community.

Animation: Show a before and after of a community going from bad to good

To learn more and donate, go to www.Entrepreneursoftheworld.com to get started.

Animation: Show the logo and have the website appear under it

There you have it. The storyboard doesn't have to be anything special; you just need a plan. Most times, while I am storyboarding my video, I'm still watching animated videos made by bigger companies to get inspiration for my visuals like I did for my script. Not only does it give me ideas, but it gets my brain going to thinking about things that I do not see in the videos I'm watching.

I am looking for things like the flow of their animations, transitions, brand colors, etc. I also want to keep an open mind to discover things that I may not have thought of. Imagine you are building a house. You need a blueprint of what the house is going to look like. The script and storyboard are going to be a part of your blueprint. Remember, the script is your foundation; you need to make sure it is solid so people can be safe inside and they can stay longer. In other words, you want to *make* sure they stay in the house.

Your visuals are like the exterior and design of the house. It will attract them to the house and make them tell their friends how beautiful and well-constructed the house is.

After I finish the scripting and storyboarding, it is time to execute by putting the video together. It doesn't have to be exactly like the storyboard because more likely than not, you will get better ideas as you are making the video. Not only is that acceptable, but it is preferred that you go with those ideas. Once you get the first draft of your video together, you want to watch the video over and over and polish it up and revise any mistakes. You are always going to mess up after your first draft.

That is why there is a step dedicated to editing the video. You can put your full focus into making sure the video is perfect for release and portraying the message that you want it to portray. Watch the video repeatedly and even get other eyes on the video to check for mistakes that you may have missed. This is the entire process that I go through when creating an animated video.

You should use this process even if you are having someone make the video for you.

This will help everything go smoothly and effectively communicate the message, impact, and results you want your video to have.

I know that we spent way more time on the planning side of the video than the execution side. This is because there is a lot of technical stuff when explaining how to make the animated video and how to use the software that I use. Also, in this chapter, we are focused on how to tell your story using animation. Therefore, the focus is on the planning, but if you are interested in learning how to make animated videos yourself, I did not leave you hanging. I created a crash course that you can find at

www.learnanimationbootcamp.com.

It will show you how to use the software and create an animated video. It goes further by taking you through the entire process I go through when creating my video. Remember, I also make animated videos if you don't want to make them for yourself.

Pros and cons of hiring someone vs. doing it yourself

There are two ends of the spectrum when deciding whether to hire someone to do your animated video(s) or do them yourself. I am going to talk about what both sides look like while pointing out their pros and cons. Then I'll bring up situations where both sides are important and my advice on doing either one. I want to begin by saying I am not biased to one or the other. My company offers both, so I don't have to play favorites. Here are the pros and cons of both.

Making your own:

Pro

- Cost-effective in the long run

- Complete control over how the video turns out

- Opportunity to have more content

Cons

- Complete control over how the video turns out (if you don't know what to do)

- Not as cost-effective in the short run

- It takes time to learn the process and software

Hiring someone to create the video for you:

Pro

- Cost-effective in the short run

- A professional to walk you through the steps and use experience

- The hands-off approach saves time

Con

- Not cost-effective in the long run

- It can be costly if you want multiple videos

- It can be difficult to communicate the exact vision you see in your head

Now let's go through each part of the pros and cons and talk about them a bit. If you are making your own video, it can be cost-effective in the long run because the cost of the video once you buy the software is almost nothing. That means you can make as many videos as you want without paying each time - not including if you pay for an outside person to do the voiceover. This option opens the door for you to have as much animated content as you want.

This decision also allows you to run free with your creative ideas and change them as you see fit. This *only* works if you know what you are doing and have a strategy. If you follow the process we just went through, you shouldn't have a problem.

On the flip side, this can be bad if you do not know what to do. Which, at that point, it can become very time-consuming. It will also take time to learn the software and process, and it will take time to create and edit the video. That is time that you could use for something else, so you will have to decide if you have the time to learn and then create videos.

Another downside is that it may not be worth it if you are just planning to have one or two videos. Not just because of the price, because it still can be a little bit cheaper than hiring someone. But you also have to think about the time you are spending learning to create the video, then the time spent actually creating the video and then editing it. Is it worth it for one or two videos? That is something you will need to ask yourself.

Now let's look at the pros and cons of getting someone to create videos for you. On the upside, this option is cost-effective in the short run. If you are only getting one or two videos, you don't have to spend the time learning, creating, and editing the video. You can just get someone to whip the video up for you. If you go with a professional that makes animated videos, then they can easily walk you through the steps and everything they need from you.

They will know how to make everything easier. Remember, the point of hiring someone is to save yourself stress and time. A professional will make it as stress-free as possible so you can do other things. On the other side, it will be the complete opposite if you don't hire a professional. It can add more stress, take up your time, you still have to pay, and you may not even get the video you were hoping for; So you have to be cautious about that.

If your organization has a person that focuses strictly on the marketing side, then I would get them to learn how to make animated videos. If you want a series of videos or more than three or four videos, it may be worth looking into making videos yourself to have regular content. But if you are the only one in your organization and wear many hats, I would recommend hiring a professional.

The only exception would be if you have a tight budget, then I would learn how to make animated videos and focus on using animated videos to market your organization. This is why we made our crash course that teaches people how to make animated videos quickly. So not only do you learn quickly, but you learn in a way that you can *make* animated videos quickly, so it doesn't take up too much of your time. The best thing to do is sit down and list out your company goals and plans. Then decide which one is best for you.

Different ways to use videos

There are many ways that you can use animated videos to advertise your organization, and we will go over some now. The first is taking your target audience through a process down a planned path. The proper term would be a sales funnel. For example, with our example nonprofit, we would be targeting donors. So first, we would attract their attention on social media with an introduction video about our organization and what we do. The goal is to peak their interest and have them follow our social media page to start seeing more of our content.

Then the next video would discuss the different programs that we have and general information about them. We want to see if there is a program that they relate to and would want to go to our website to learn more about that specific program. This way is perfect to attract new people to your marketing space so they can see more of you. This will lead to the second way videos can be used as valuable content. The idea here is to be a source of valuable information. In other words, you want to put out information relating to the people that you are serving, so they are learning new things from you. This will build you up to be an expert in the field. It builds trust and a reputation for your organization. The key here is to do it consistently.

Take our example nonprofit organization. Since we are helping entrepreneurs and small business owners, we will be dropping tips that many people may not know. Information about setting up a business, marketing a business, reasons businesses fail, things you may not know, etc. This will bring more people to the page, it will keep the people we already have coming back, and again we will be an expert in the field.

When they have an issue in the industry that they need help with, they will come to us. My goal is to become a resource for them to learn new things that can take them further. This will help them build trust and credibility in my organization.

The third way to use videos is as regular content. The goal of this content is to stay on your audience's mind. I truly believe in the saying out of sight, out of mind. This is why I believe big establishments like McDonald's, Nike, and Apple still advertise. So, with our nonprofit, we will post animated characters standing in front of our logo, short clips of animated characters starting their business, and more. The point is to stay on our follower's minds, and with animation, it can be an original way for them to remember you. Remember, animation helps you stand out!

A personal note from TJ:

I appreciate you reading my chapter, and I hope that it helped you get at least two steps closer to reaching your goals. In my chapter, I touched on creating animation and its benefits. I didn't want to just give you that information and then leave you stranded. If you go to the website: www.learnanimationbootcamp.com, there is a free course that you can take that will teach you how to make animated videos. I will show you how to use the software, go over the steps I take when making a video, and you can also watch along as I make a video. It is an informative course that you can finish in a few days with spending only an hour at most each day. I even include some activities to help you practice what I show you.

Another gift I want to give you for reading my chapter is 25% off an animated video order. Just send me the code: "BIN MARKETING" to my email, any of my social media platforms, or even through my website: www.TJsAnimationWorkshop.com.

P.S. Feel free to share that code with any of your friends; it is highly encouraged. Thank you again for reading my chapter, and I would love to hear from you.

Karen KJ Johnson

www.kjsdstudio.com

kjsdstudio@gmail.com

Karen KJ Johnson is a Global Brand Strategist and Founder & CEO of KJ Strategy Design Studio, a brand development consultancy, and The Brand I Academy, a professional development learning center specializing in branding, marketing & sales. KJ is on a mission to help African American women entrepreneurs & executive directors build a brand of higher purpose by helping them to fully own their cultural identity, rock their self-confidence & showcase their brilliance to the world.

KJ has over 25 years of business experience in both the nonprofit and for-profit sectors. She has received numerous awards, accolades and nominations for her work, including being named as one of the 2021 "50 Powerful Women in Business to Know" by WOD Media Magazine, 2021 "25 Global Influencer" by K.I.S.H. Magazine, 2020 "Top 100 Businesswomen to follow on LinkedIn, featured in The NGO Whisperer TM Magazine, featured in the 2020 Today's Purpose Woman Magazine & calendar, graced the cover of Influential Digital Magazine and named as one of the 2019 "Top 25 Purpose Driven Woman to Watch" by TPW just to name a few.

KJ partners with several nonprofit organizations, serving as the Master Brand Strategist for the award-winning, The NGO Whisperer TM and Faculty Member, Head of Branding & Marketing for The NGO Whisperer TM Global Fellowship, based out of the U.K. KJ was recently appointed as a Board Member & Program Director for Dress for Success-Dallas. She hosts her weekly radio show, The Brand I Am. Her other projects include writing her next book, "Your Business Don't Have a Brand," and launching an online branding & marketing school. KJ currently resides in Dallas, TX, has a brilliant grown son, Chester, a beautiful glam-daughter, Legacee, and yes, you guessed it…she's an avid Dallas Cowboy's fan!

For more information, follow her:

Website:

https://www.kjsdstudio.com

LinkedIn:

https://www.linkedin.com/company/kjsdstudio

https://www.linkedin.com/in/karen-kj-johnson

Instagram:

https://www.instagram.com/kjsdstudio

https://www.instagram.com/thebrandiacademy

Facebook:

https://www.facebook.com/karenr.johnson.750

https://www.facebook.com/kjsdstudio

https://www.facebook.com/thebrandiamshow

The Heart of the Matter

We all know the heart is an amazing organ. In fact, if it stops functioning, the body begins to systematically shut down. The heart is the power source of the body. The heart has four chambers for circulating blood. The upper chambers- called the right & left atriums - collect blood flowing in from the body and in from the lungs. The lower chambers – called right & left ventricles- collect blood from the atria then forcefully pumps blood to the lungs.

The blood provides the body with the oxygen and nutrients it needs. It also takes the body's waste products away from the tissues, thus sustaining life. Without it, nothing in the body can work, including the brain. The heart creates electoral pulses that run through the body, supplying energy to everything. If the power source, the heart, is turned off, not only will the body begin to shut down, but it will also start to die.

Now that I have your attention let us talk about the *"heart"* of nonprofits.

Branding may not be the first thing that comes to mind as a priority for a nonprofit, social business, or any other organization that focuses on delivering social impact. In fact, most nonprofits would say branding is for those big "for-profits" corporations. "*We don't have that kind of budget for creativity.*" "*We have more purposeful goals that impact lives that we must focus on.*" "*We exist to serve a purpose, not to make a profit.*" "*We actually have a logo,*" etc.

What does brand mean, anyway?

This is the million-dollar question. Often when brand is discussed its referenced as a logo imprinted. Logos are the #1 visual element we think of when it comes to branding. It is a major part of what draws a consumer to an organization. While a logo and other visual elements make up a brand, the brand has a higher purpose. That purpose is the "why," and the "why" pulls at the heartstrings, inspiring others to act.

The higher business of purpose is about making an emotional connection. Brand is the way an organization is perceived by those who experience it.

Branding is the power source for a nonprofit, social business, or any service-based small business. It is the heart that pumps blood that carries the oxygen and nutrients throughout the organization. It is the power source that aligns the internal identity and external image with its values and mission. When an organization's board of directors, staff, and volunteers receive the oxygen and nutrients, it creates cohesion, focus, and clarity, positioning the organization for credibility and trust between its beneficiaries, strategic partners, and donors.

Identify Your Brand Heart

Purpose

In order for the organization to survive, the purpose, vision, mission, values, and goals must be identified. These are the nutrients and oxygen that are required to survive. Let us first start with purpose. There are numerous reasons why nonprofits are started. Whether it is a general sense of helping others or someone close has been personally affected, wanting to contribute to solving a problem, or wanting to organize financial resources toward a cause, it is important to define a purpose.

When a purpose is defined and aligned with a greater cause, the organization will have an uncanny ability to inspire financial support, attract talented board members, influence strategic partnerships & above all, impact beneficiaries.

Brand purpose is a higher reason as to why your nonprofit exist, other than to make a profit. The goal is to give people a purpose, a cause to champion, or a reason to believe so they feel inspired to come to the board meetings, put in the work, and have beneficiaries take advantage of the services offered. Having a purpose will unite the board members & staff and foster a deeper connection with the audience.

When defining a purpose, answer the following questions:

- Why am I starting this nonprofit, or why do we exist?
- What wrong are we trying to make right?
- Why is this important?

A vision is an effective statement that ensures the entire organization is working toward the same shared idea(s) about where the organization is headed. Your vision needs to be big enough that both the challenge and possibility of achieving it are audacious and intimidating. Although the vision should be bold, achieving it needs to be a possibility so that the team believes and buys into that vision. So, having some clarity on where the organization is going will help the board make more meaningful decisions and think more strategically.

This is because if a certain action points towards the organization's future, then the organization is much more likely to stay "on brand" and on track.

To help create a vision statement, ask:

- Where are you now? (In terms of business metrics)

- What future do we want to help create & achieve? In 5 years? In 10 years?

Mission

A mission statement describes the organization's function, targeted audience(s), and competitive advantages. It is a short statement of goals and philosophies. It defines what the organization is, why it exists, and its reason for being. It tells others what the organization does, who it serves, and how they are served. The mission statement is the driving force for everything you want to ultimately achieve.

To create an effective mission statement, answer:

- How do we strategically create the future outlined in the vision during our day-to-day operations?

Core Values

Core values are the operating philosophies or principles that guide the organization's conduct both internally and externally. Your values stand at the very core of your brand. You want to determine how you want your brand to be perceived in the market. This is about how you DO things, so it's more about the experience that your beneficiaries, strategic partners, board members, staff, and the wider public will have interacting with your brand.

Core values are in support and pursuit of the mission, vision, and purpose. Best practice is to select 3 – 5 values.

Questions to answer:

- How will we govern ourselves?
- What are our non-negotiables?

The Pulse of the Heart

Targeted Audience

Without a clear idea of who you are trying to educate, inspire, impact, or influence, you will fail to deliver meaningful, useful, and valuable content needed and wanted based on the targeted audiences' aspirations or problems. Identifying your audience helps you intimately understand the problem they have, the issues that affect them, their goals, and how your product and services will benefit them. It is important to know the details of your targeted audience in order to resonate with them. Being able to do so will allow the organization to pull at the heartstrings through an emotional connection which is the initiator and driver of attraction.

Here are a few components to consider:

1. Pain Point(s)

2. Age group

3. Gender

4. What do they fear as a result of the problem(s)?

5. What emotions & feelings do they experience as a result of the problem?

Position

Brand positioning is defining a distinctive place in the mind of the targeted audience(s). It describes how the organization is different from your competitors. A branding positioning strategy involves creating how you want the organization to be perceived in a specific way in the consumers' mind. When determining a brand's position, you must understand what the customer wants, the capabilities of the organization and understand the competitors' positioning. Do not use generic words such as quality-products, successful or unique... this is the aim of every brand. The key is to set the organization apart from the competitor(s) and secure a spot in the mind of the consumers.

Communication

Your brand messaging is the one thing that connects every piece of content you create. Brand messaging refers to the underlying value proposition conveyed, and the language & tone used in the content. Any content created is a message of your brand. So, when you craft your messages, think about the positioning, key benefits, values, targeted audience, and tone of voice. When communicating, ensure the organization is speaking directly to its' targeted audience. When communicating in general terms, you won't pull at the heartstrings, which is the key to emotionally connect. Together, these elements define the overall "key" message that guides your marketing efforts.

Goals

Goals describe what an organization expects to accomplish with its branding over a specific period of time. Before deciding on your brand goal(s), ask what you are trying to achieve through branding. Brand goals are similar to business goals; however, they are slightly different.

There are five major brand goals:

- Build awareness.

- Create an emotional connection.

- Differentiate your offering.

- Create credibility & trust.

- Motivate purchase or donation.

Let's look at each one.

- **Brand awareness**. This means to increase your brand recognition. With this strategy and goal in mind, a nonprofit is trying to reach as many people as it can. An increase in brand awareness causes individuals to recall, recognize and remember the nonprofit.

- **Creating an emotional connection**. This is all about story-telling that resonates with the targeted audience and describes the WHY and the evolution of making an impact on those serviced.

- **Differentiating your products or services**. This is about separating the nonprofit from similar nonprofits. What value are you offering that is uniquely different from the others?

- **Creating credibility & trust**. A nonprofit needs to look professional and appealing to potential beneficiaries. Building solid relationships can develop a deeper level of trust. Whatever you say you are going to do, you must follow through—being consistent in-person and online builds trust.

- **Motivate purchasing and donations**. This can be achieved by creating a trusted reputation, delivering more than what is expected, and being visible as a leader making an impact.

The Beauty of the Heart

Personality

Brand personality is all about humanizing the organization and communicate consistently through all content. The brand personality is a consistent set of traits that a specific targeted audience or segment of people enjoy and can relate to. This personality is a qualitative value-add that a brand gains in addition to its functional benefits. The brand personality elicits an emotional response with the intention of inciting positive actions that benefit the organization. Your brand personality sets the tone for the overall experience.

There are generally five types of brand personalities with common traits:

1. **Excitement-** carefree, spirited.

2. **Sincerity-** kindness, thoughtfulness & orientation toward family values.

3. **Ruggedness-** rough, tough, outdoorsy.

4. **Competence:** successful, accomplished & intelligent, highlighted by leadership.

5. **Sophistication:** elegant, prestigious.

Don't just select one of the above common personalities. Make sure the personality you select represents you and the organization.

Here are a few questions to help guide you in identifying the personality of the organization:

- When people interact with your brand, how do you want them to feel?

- What adjectives would you use to describe your brand?

Brand voice is all about the words and language you use and the tone in which those words are delivered. It plays a critical role in the organization's communication. It is important for the consumer to be able to recognize the voice and tone of your organization as it sets you apart from others conducting the same type of work. If your voice and tone appear to change frequently, it becomes challenging for the consumer to know exactly what your organization is about. Voice describes your organization's personality and can position you as an authoritative source for your area of expertise. Tone is the emotional inflection applied to the voice. Voice must remain consistent; however, tone will adjust based on what's suitable for a particular message.

Here are a few things to think about when determining the voice of your organization:

- Review the organization's mission statement.
- Know your audience (which could change based on the message you are delivering).

Logo

Logos are the #1 visual element we think of when it comes to branding. It is a major part of what draws a consumer to your nonprofit. The logo represents your overall image, and it shows the consumer who you are. It is the #1 visual element that will attract the consumer to you. Your logo gets not only the consumer excited but also your board members, staff, and volunteers. Your logo speaks volumes and showcases the strength and professionalism of your organization. Logos are not to be designed before you establish the foundation. Think about a logo like you would about the interior design for a new home...It is not executed until the house is built.

Typeface

This is not just about selecting and using a particular font. All typographic elements should be arranged properly in your design, the visual arrangement, color contrast, the size, everything. These elements impact the design on both a big and small scale. In simple terms, typography is the style and the way a text is presented. When you are developing the heart, a persistent heartbeat of fonts should be used.

This particular rhythm helps the organization express the personality of the heart. It represents the tone and values of the brand just like the color palette represents a feeling or visually represents an emotional connection. Typography sets the mood. It works silently. But just because it is quiet does not mean it is not making an impact. It is conveying a message and can easily change perceptions. Typography is an art form that can alter the significance of what is being communicated. Be strategic when selecting fonts.

Color Palette

Colors, like features, follow the changes of the emotions.

- Pablo Picasso

Emotions are powerful and drive the decision-making process. It is important to cultivate a strong emotional connection with the consumers. How consumers <u>feel</u> about a brand has more pull than what they <u>think</u> about a brand. And when you pair that with emotion your brand colors provide, it has the ability to impact your sales, performance & donations even more than the products you offer.

Typically, you want to select no more than three colors. Keep the emotional message clear & concise. Use your branding colors in your logo, website, storefront, marketing materials, apparel, advertisement, social media, etc. This consistency strengthens your nonprofit's brand & awareness. Select colors that represent the identity of the nonprofit and that attract the targeted audience(s).

Photography

There is a study that states we as humans process images 60,000 times faster than we do text/words, and 90% of information transmitted to the brain is visual. Human beings are visual creatures. Photography helps to tell the brand story and emotionally connect. Photography is the first visual element (after the logo) that will make a first impression. You only have seven seconds to make that impression. Photography allows you the ability to better capture the impact your nonprofit is making on the beneficiaries. Consistently displaying high-quality photos helps builds brand trust and recognition.

Sidebar: Ensure all Board members and staff have professional headshots to utilize on the organization's website and marketing materials. NO EXCEPTIONS.

Keeping the Heart Alive

Maintaining a Healthy Brand Heart

In order to improve life's chances of living a long enjoyable, stress-free life, there are things you should work on every day to keep your heart healthy. The heart can't function properly if you don't take the necessary precautions to keep it in excellent shape. Typically, there are five areas to help you maintain a healthy heart. 1) a healthy diet, 2) regular physical activity, 3) quit smoking, 4) control your cholesterol, and 5) control your blood pressure. The Heart of your nonprofit needs attention every day. It's the organ that breathes life into your organization. As your organization scales, grows, changes, and succeeds, the heart must follow suit. The brand heart is susceptible to external factors like news, trends, and current events. We live in a world where news media outlets, influencers, and social media influence every narrative. It's important for you to take control of your heart and tell your brand story.

Maintaining a healthy heart will require consistency. To ensure consistency, it becomes critically important for you to document your brand heart guidelines and share them with your board members, staff, and volunteers. As the CEO and/or Executive Director, it is important that you reiterate the mission, goals, and message. It is important that all decisions are in alignment with the values of the organization. Conduct routine checks for brand inconsistencies and correct them when necessary.

I recommend that you trademark your business name. It is the primary identity of your organization. By owning the rights to your brand name, you have better leverage over unauthorized use and any competitors who attempt to copy or steal your brand. When possible secure the domain and social media pages of the brand name. This will further advance the consistency and help consumers, donors, and strategic partners discover, follow, and support the organization.

Your logo, color palette & fonts represent the overall feel of the organization's brand. Incorporate them into every marketing material and digital platform, such as websites, social media sites, blogs, etc. Consistency builds credibility, trust, attracts, and converts.

All of your marketing - website, social media platforms, and advertising must represent your brand. Millions of people access the internet, and billions are on social media daily. These potential donors, beneficiaries, volunteers, staff, and/or potential board members will research first before actually reaching out to the organization. Make sure all of these channels are in alignment.

The board members, staff, and volunteers represent the organization at all times. Have each board member, staff, and volunteer develop an elevator pitch. This will help assist in making sure everyone is speaking the same key message. Ensure they represent the best of who the organization is by conducting routine checks and reiterating the organization's mission & goals. Create a brand scorecard of the brand goals and use it regularly to ensure the heart pumps as it has been designed to do.

The heart is an amazing organ, and when properly cared for it will sustain you, allowing the organization to positively impact the lives of many. Properly caring for the heart reduces the chances of heart failure and, best of all, prevents the need for a heart transplant.

Made in the USA
Monee, IL
10 September 2021